ALL MIRACLE

Morning Song

April 9, 1924–February 16, 1999

ALL MIRACLE

Morning Song

Poems by
Elizabeth B. Rooney

Edited by
Patricia M. Rooney

Brigham Farm
Publishing

Brigham Farm
Publishing

In loving memory of you,
dearest Momma

ALL MIRACLE SERIES

Elizabeth B. Rooney

Morning Song

Packages

Storing September

Gift Wrapped

Contents

March

April

May

Preface

This series of books is for all of Elizabeth Rooney's family, friends and fans who have been patiently awaiting the publication of her collected poems and for all those who will meet her for the first time in these pages.

Elizabeth Brigham Rooney, my mother, began writing poems in the summer of 1978. Before her death in February 1999, she had written over seven hundred of them, interspersed amongst the prose entries in her journals like bursts of song.

She was more surprised than anyone at this sudden and abundant release of creativity, although she'd been encouraged from her youth to pursue a career in writing. Raised by highly literate parents, she attended and excelled at top-notch schools, yet protested, "I don't have anything to say!"

Later, she came to realize the creative flow had been blocked, among other things, by fear of failing those who expected so much from her. It wasn't until she made a complete surrender to the One who had placed the love of poetry inside her that she was free, not only to write but also to embrace all of life as a holy gift.

This "total commitment," as she described it, came as she was preparing to be inducted into the Society of the Companions of the Holy Cross, a lay order of Episcopal women. She already had her masters in Christian Education and was married to an Episcopal priest, yet there was something missing.

"For years I'd been an active Christian adult and before that, a rather timid, but believing child. I prayed quite regularly for as long as I can remember, but at the same time stayed a safe distance from the cross. To embrace the cross wholeheartedly requires an act of will. To my astonishment, the result was an absolute flooding of joy. I had fallen in love with God. It was as if my veins were bubbling with champagne and the poems began to flow freely, coming as delightful surprises day after day."

The first one to come was "Adelynrood," named for the retreat center in Massachusetts where the encounter took place.

Adelynrood

The winter of my heart
Melts here.
Rivulets run
Beneath the ice of fear.

Pierced by your warmth,
Life moves.
Spring has begun.
I feel the sun, the sun!

8/11/78

As her newly awakened faith grew, so did the conviction that
these poems were gifts to be shared. She summoned the courage
to exchange poetry with friends who were fellow writers. Then
she attended a workshop led by the poet Luci Shaw and there
found a kindred heart and mind, a friend and mentor, who even-
tually introduced her to the reading public in a way Elizabeth
never dreamed possible.

Luci had been asked to write a chapter in an upcoming book
entitled *Bright Legacy, Portraits of Ten Outstanding Christian Women*
about someone she "particularly admired." As Luci explains in
her chapter, "Rather then telling of the impact on my life of an
internationally known personality, I felt a growing conviction
that I would rather talk about someone like Elizabeth Rooney, an
'ordinary' woman, hardly known beyond her own circle of friends
and colleagues, though uniquely gifted by God. Her experience
would, I was sure, suggest to other women with earthbound, un-
remarkable lives that he could lift the most mundane existence
into his own bright beauty and glory. What he requires are eyes
open to his brightness and ears alert for his voice."

Luci's words so aptly describe the gift Elizabeth received at
Adelynrood. She had indeed been given "eyes open to his brightness and ears alert for his voice." And so the woman who had
protested she had nothing to write about, was able to declare, "I
know what I want to say. . . . I want to write about God, about the
intense tenderness manifest in the world wherever goodness,
truth and beauty allow it to shine through… Today in the park-
ing lot there was a puddle—a muddy, shallow puddle on the
blacktop, not more than an inch deep at best and perhaps four
feet across. When looked at from a certain angle, it reflected all

the treetops in it, and clouds and sky, all the way to infinity. I think I'm like the puddle—muddy, shallow, insignificant—but, by God's grace, capable of the miracle of reflecting him, and in him, all the wonder of the universe.

"The more I become aware of the active presence of God, the more beautiful and sacred everything becomes.... Do we need miracles, or do we need only to perceive that every ordinary thing around us is already miraculous?"

My mother's hope, as voiced in the following prayer by an unknown author, was that her poems might open other eyes to His brightness and other ears to His voice, that they would come to understand as she had that "Life is *all* miracle."

"Days pass and the years vanish and we walk sightless among miracles. Lord, fill our eyes with seeing and our minds with knowing. Let there be moments when your Presence, like lightning, illumines the darkness in which we walk. Help us to see, wherever we gaze, that the bush burns unconsumed. And we, clay touched by God, will reach out for holiness and exclaim in wonder, 'How filled with awe is this place and we did not know it.'"

« »

This series, *All Miracle*, includes four volumes, *Morning Song*, *Packages*, *Storing September*, and *Gift Wrapped*, which correspond to spring, summer, autumn, and winter. Those who, like my mother, have grown up on farms or in the country understand and interpret life, in large part, by the passage of the seasons. Her poetry is characterized by a deep awareness of life's interconnectedness and the yearly cycles of death and rebirth. After much reading and rereading of the poems, I felt the most natural way to group them would be by these intrinsic themes, which include not only the four seasons but also the parallel seasons of human life, such as childhood, adulthood, aging, and death and the corresponding seasons of the liturgical year, such as Advent, Christmas, Lent, and Easter. Although each poem is meant to be read and savored on its own, the groupings are intended to accentuate their collective rhythm and flow.

—*Patricia M. Rooney*

Acknowledgments

My most sincere thanks to the following persons and companies:

To all who helped launch this publishing venture by generously contributing to the Elizabeth B. Rooney Memorial Poetry Fund.

To Eugenia Brown, who so cheerfully volunteered hours and hours of typing.

To Louise Summers, Delores Topliff, Pat Hitchcock, Norma Madsen, Sharol Hayner, Joyce Young, Kimberly Linyard, Janice Griffin, and Sr. Peronne-Marie Thiebert, for their gracious help with proofreading.

To my brother Mark, for all of his encouragement, advice, and nagging.

To the wonderful folks at Impressions Book and Journal Services, Inc., especially John Ferguson, Mary Boss, and Elizabeth Ragsdale, for their expertise, enthusiasm, and genuine interest in this project. Your patience and warmth working with a first-time publisher made all the difference.

To Kevin Wasowski and Jane Landen of Edwards Brothers, for their kind and professional help.

Spring

This spring has a curious under-girding feeling of hope... maybe it's because spring really does seem to be arriving and last winter was so long and so dire that I had begun to develop a pagan despair of ever having the sun warm us properly again and consequently now enjoy a pagan rapture over every harbinger of spring—every speck of warmth and greenness and blossom and song... and yet the real source of hope and joy lies beyond all this in the knowledge of God's continuing and omnipresent caring and love for each one of us... this knowledge of being held in the hollow of His hand, of all that ever was being held in the hollow of His hand,... this knowledge is, I think, the basis of the springing hope which goes with me daily.

Journal, 4/6/78

Morning Song

Praised be God
For the glory of morning,
For trees in the leafing
Of spring time adorning,
For song pouring forth,
For each bird and his call,
For the light of God's heaven,
Illumining all.
Praised be God
For His mercy, His might,
His joy in creating
All things that delight.

5/26/84

March

Morning in March

Today's a day for kites,
For things that soar—
For spirits and for hawks
And songs of praise.

Everything longs to fly—
Shingles, the flag,
The laundry on the line,
Old leaves, small boys.

All kinds
Of tied-down things
Are pulling hard
And straining at their strings.

Old mother earth, let go!
They will come back
After a turn or two
Around the sky.

But right now
Sun, wind, spring—
Oh, everything—
Keep calling them to fly!

3/13/82

Dandelion

Hope is one small, bedraggled, muddy flower
Blooming before its time
And somehow meaning more
Than all the mountains of residual winter
Stretching around us.

3/10/79

Gray Day

Gentle, healing, quiet, cool—
Fog-wrapped sky and sky-filled pool.
Branches reaching to caress
Lie within the quietness.
Folk, whose feet go flapping by,
Don't the puddles catch your eye?

2/4/59

March

I hear the growl of the thunder,
I feel the lash of the rain.
My truck is stuck in the driveway.
It will soon be snowing again.

The mud is up to the hub caps.
The fog is clammy and cold.
The barnyard is dank with manure
And spring is three days old.

3/29/79

When?

When will it come,
The spring I cannot meet?
I, who have always gone
On questing feet
To find the pussy willow by the stream,
The first pasque flowers in the prairie grass,
The shy hepaticas among the leaves?

When will I not be there
To stand heart hungry
In the cold March wind
And hear the red wings cry?
When will I fail to see
The maple's swelling buds
Against the sky?

When will I die?

1/14/88

Challenge

Trust Him
As if you were a daffodil
Thrusting your vulnerable green
Into the cold March air.
He has called you
To love and praise Him here
In this strange modern scene.
He knows more than you know
About the pain
Of being human
And the cost of sin.
He knows the wind is chill,
The snow half melted
And the ground still bare.
And yet, He calls like spring,
"Come, follow me!"
Be like the daffodils
And dare!

3/23/88

Quaker Meeting

Enter within the center
Where the will is still,
Where the mind can find
A kind of quietness.

The most beautiful things in the world
Happen in perfect silence.
Sunlight touches our earth silently.
Seeds stir in rebirth silently.
Babies grow in the womb silently.
Blossoms break into bloom silently.

And when we are perfectly still,
Perfectly open to his will,
Our Lord comes silently.

3/20/59

Waiting

Lie quietly, my soul!
This narrow space beneath the earth
Does not admit
Much movement or much air.
Be patient
While the husks of self
Disintegrate around you.
Presently,
You will know
Whether or not the long years in the sun
Produced a kernel of integrity
Able to grow again
Toward warmth and light.
Be still
And trust the night
And trust the light.

1/1/80

Potato Poem

In the closed closet
Where you sleep,
The dark is constant,
Close and deep.
The early bright
Epiphany
Of spring's first light
Is hidden from you,
Yet you sprout.
Heaped in the corner
Dark and dumb,
How can you tell
The time has come?

At this, potato,
Ever wise,
To his inquisitor replies,
"You are forgetting
We have eyes!"

1/24/96

Chimney Swifts

The chimney swifts cut patterns in the sky.
They snip, snip, snip
Great soaring circles of the hanging blue
And carry them away to line their nests
So fledgling chimney swifts,
Born in the dark, soot-blinded,
Will be reminded of the sky
And know which way to go
When they begin to fly.

6/11/79

Surprise

The night before,
We went to bed
All innocent of spring—
No rising tumult in the heart,
Just winter slumbering.

We woke to find the daffodils,
A sudden yellow shout
Of new-sprung love
Across the hills
And spring was all about.

3/17/88

Visitor

I opened the door
And spring came in,
Tousled my hair
And tickled my chin,
Blew all my papers
Across the floor.
Spring came in
When I opened the door.

4/29/85

Spring Comes Marching

Spring comes marching
Over the hill,
With crocus and snowdrop
And daffodil.

Redwings and robins
Have scouted the farm,
Watching the snowdrifts
Of winter disarm.

There's a hatching of moths
On the window pane
And the peepers are piping in
Spring again.

The flowering army
Springs from the ground
At the peeper's sound,
At the peeper's sound.

3/29/86

Snowdrops

The bell chimes.
Silver notes
Shimmer across
Each garden and each field.
Caught
In the cool of spring
Their music has congealed.
Clusters of small white blossoms
Everywhere
Shaped like the sound of bells
Have fallen from the air.

2/14/87

Tulips

Spring's lighted tulip candles
Everywhere.
Their bright flames flare
In little gardens
And the courthouse square.
The warm sun
Reached the hidden bulbs,
Ignited
Their fires of joy,
And set our world alight
With their brave blossoms
So we could delight.

5/4/91

For St. Patrick

Oh, olivaceous,
Glaucous, berylline,
Virescent, emerald,
Aquamarine!
Oh, green, green, green!
Apple and algae,
Shamrock, bottle, pea,
Grass, leaf, and Irish,
Malachite and sea!
How green,
How greatly, greenly, greenish green!

When earth began,
Was there green fire
Within the heart
Of God's desire?

3/3/81

Ireland

The land is rich
With silences and seas,
The greenness of it
Strewn with ancient stones.
This place was holy once,
Is holy still.

Broken and scarred
By famine, conquest, rape,
Its roofless ruins gape
Beneath its grieving skies.
Passion dies slowly here.
Old blood
Still cries for vengeance,
And old prayers
Still rise.

3/20/91

Homesick

I stood before a hill in Ireland once—
Close-cropped, rock strewn,
A short, steep Irish hill,
No mountain this.
Yet such a hill, it seems,
Could cut off half the Western sky
And rob a man
Of courage, hope and dreams.
I felt as though I too were thrall
To some deep magic in the Irish soil
That would have held me there
Or called me home
No matter where I sailed
Or tried to roam.
However rich and famous I became
In some far place,
That Irish hillside would have called my name
And wooed me back again
To its scarred face.

3/20/94

Inheritance

I wonder if she ever shed her tears,
That Irish grandmother
Whose husband starved,
Whose daughters stayed behind
Or died at sea,
Whose three small sons she gave
To strangers
To be cared for properly.
She disappeared. . . .
They say she left no trace,
But all the tears she wept
Or swallowed silently
Still rise in me.
Perhaps that's why
I cry so easily.

3/20/91

Dying in Springtime

It seems a most ironic contrast, this—
To waste away
Just as the world grows bright.
Bedridden though I am,
I feel the spring.
I see the sticky buds
Swell on the trees,
Hear robins,
Welcome friends with daffodils.
All the remembered thrills
Of loving life
Live in me as I die.
I want to savor every day
Of sweetness
Spring can offer me this year.
For when spring comes again
I won't be here.

3/23/89

Lord of Life

Lord of the robin
And the daffodil,
We thank you
For the swelling buds of spring.

You, who loved beauty into being,
Who made spring,
How could you bring yourself
To drink of death
In a green garden
Where the very breath
Of every growing thing
Cried out life's goodness
And the joy of living?

You, who are life itself,
How could you bear to die?
Yet, you found courage
To surrender life to death
And by your giving,
Carried us all past death
Into your world
Of everlasting living.

3/22/98

Grandmother

Did Jesus know his grandmother?
Did the child come
And scramble in her lap
And cuddle there?
Did he bring treasures to her—
Colored stones and lilies of the field?
And did she help him learn
The legends of his people's history?
Did they watch moon rise
And the stars his Father made?
We have no word about her being there,
Can only hope that she was near
To soothe a small boy's hurts,
To help him wash his feet
And smooth his hair.

7/25/96

Jesus

It's a long time now
But, yes,
I saw him once.
He wasn't bigger
Than the other men
But he had a kind of strength,
A vigor, a vitality, a joy . . .
I was just a boy
There by the side of the road
When the crowd came by
But I still remember him
Swinging along with his friends.
There was something about him
Made you feel like singing.
It's a long time now
But, yes,
I saw him once.

1/4/87

One of Us

A poor man works in a carpenter's shop,
Works till his back hurts,
Doesn't stop
Just because he is hot or sweaty or tired.
He works to eat, not to be admired.

A poor man eats what his work will earn—
Loaves and fishes. He doesn't spurn
Wine in its season. A poor man's glad
To have shared with his friends
All the food he had.

A poor man sleeps where his day's work ends—
By the side of the road,
At the home of friends.
In the back of a boat on a stormy sea
A poor man sleeps luxuriously.

A poor man dies, as poor men die,
With his helpless family standing by
And none to defend him from the cry
Of "Crucify him! Crucify!"

8/21/81

For Real

Gethsemane is loneliness,
The cross is pain.
After the years of fellowship,
Of making friends, of love,
It came to this.

No glory from above,
No promised bliss
Can negate the reality
Of this, this agony,
This total gift of self,
This tenderness.

6/12/79

One, Two, Three

One time
Our Lord knelt,
Towel in hand,
Washed Peter's feet
Begrimed with sand
And, serving,
Showed
How heaven is planned.

Two times
The cock crew,
Shrill and loud
Piercing poor Peter,
Guilty, cowed.
Broken,
He stood and wept,
Head bowed.

Three times
Our Lord asked,
Three for three,
Asked Peter,
Man from Galilee,
Lovest thou Me?
Lovest thou Me?
Peter, denier,
Lovest thou Me?

3/27/86

Confrontation

When Pilate looked on Truth,
He asked Truth, "What is truth?"
But when Truth answered nothing,
Pilate tried
To flog from Truth
The truth his act denied.
Stripped, scourged and ridiculed,
Truth remained true.
Pilate, bewildered,
Let the crowd decide.
He washed his hands of Truth
And had Truth crucified.

One wonders about Pilate after that.
In the life left him
Did he still seek truth?
Or, having formed the habit of denial,
When he met Truth and Truth had him on trial,
Was he content to let his days go by
And live a lie?

5/2/81

Footprints

Dear Lord,
Who walked our world once,
You, whose feet have known
The dust of Galilee,
Cold Roman marble
And the Temple's stone,
Our God, who walked alone
The road that led to death
And through death's gates
To everlasting life,
Help us to walk toward you.
Set our feet
In your footprints, Lord,
Help us obey,
As you did,
Till we have walked
All the way.

5/27/79

Beyond Imagination

Were there only three nails, Lord,
Only one spear?
The steel that pierced
Your hands, Your feet, Your side
Was sharp with all the hatred of the years—
The bitterness, the jealousies, the fears.

We can imagine agony
But still cannot begin
To think how sin,
Thousands of years of sin,
Would wound Your spirit
As the steel Your side,
And yet it was for us
Who forged sin's steel
That You were crucified.

2/10/80

Inheritance

Oh, I am child of Adam,
Child of Cain,
With Abel's blood on me,
A spreading stain.

Cry, "Murder! Murder! Murder!"
Through the street
Of our world village
Where revenge is sweet,
And violence is encouraged
And allowed,
Even the violence
Of the mushroom cloud.

11/8/81

Hands

You hold us
In your hands
Yet put yourself,
Oh foolish Lord,
In ours.

The more fools, we
Who nail the hands
That hold us
To a tree.

6/3/83

Good Friday

If I'd been there,
Would I
Have cried out,
"Crucify!"

No,
But I would have looked
The other way—
Just as I do today.

4/1/88

Passover

How can they spread
The lamb's blood
On the lintel
Unless a lamb has died?

See at what price
He shelters us—
Our Lamb, the Crucified!

4/10/82

 *April*

April Invitation

Come with me, love,
Into the sweet and singing
Mists of spring.
The air that pierced
Is soft about us now.
The saturated earth
Moves like a living thing
Beneath our feet.
The freezing time
Is over, done, complete.
Now everything
Melts, runs, drips, gurgles,
Fills and overflows.
Come, love, and see
The new life all around us
Bursting free.

4/9/93 (Mom's Birthday)

Intermingling

How can we all be born
Of a young man's death?
Birth is the work of women.
What is this other life—
This life we reach by death,
His death and ours?
What mystery
Lies at the heart of all,
So that we taste, feel, see
Death in the midst of life
And birth on Calvary?

2/22/80

Blessing

Only the broken blesses us—
The opened seed,
The loaves and fishes shared,
The spikenard poured,
The bleeding body
Of God's son, our Lord.

4/13/81

Mary

Mother of sorrow,
Mother of joy,
You loved Him so,
This man, your boy.

You gave Him birth,
You watched Him die.
And did you never wonder why?
And did you never strive against
The will of God that made this so?

Seeing Him die, you did not know
That presently He would arise.
There is no record of your cries
Of protest.
Were there none at all?
You'd known
Ever since He was small
That soon a sword
Would pierce your heart,
Yet silently
You played your part.

Mother of sorrow,
Mother of joy,
You loved Him so,
This man, your boy.

9/15/87

Last Straw

Was it hot, Lord?
And were there dogs and flies?
We know about the dust,
The crowd, the noise,
The scourge, the thorns,
The weight of it,
The cries of ridicule.
We know about the nails
And vinegar
And finally, the spear.
But was it hot
At Golgotha that year?

9/9/78

Thieves

He died for all the thieves—
For all of us on our crosses,
Stealing the rags from one another's backs,
Robbing each other of decency and respect,
Even denying each other the right to redemption.

Life is gritty and cold
And there's never enough to go round—
Not enough wine,
Not enough loaves and fishes,
Not enough time.

Still, if we let Him, He blesses us.
The knots in the stomach unwind.
Water turns into wine,
Loaves multiply.
There is even time
In the midst of being crucified
To rediscover the Lord
Our lives have denied.

9/11/79

Facts

Life is all miracle.
The Word, enfleshed,
Moves our flesh
To find words
To praise the Word.

Imperishable Love
Shares human frailty
And by His perishing
Restores to life
Our frail humanity.

6/14/79

Crossing

We climb up time,
Moment by slipping moment,
Or slowly inch our way
Across the endlessness of space.
Everything is spread, stretched, sequential,
Near or far.

But in your cross
Time stops, space shrinks,
Infinite and eternal are conjoined
And all that ever was or will be
Meet.

Golgotha is all places everywhere,
All depth, all height,
And that one moment under Roman rule
Contains all that is past
Or is to come.

Creation and creator meet.
And time and space
Are swallowed up in love.

6/26/79

Power

Yours was a shining gentleness!
Somehow they knew—
Mary, the lepers, children, everyone.
Even the demons
Felt it gleaming through
And dared to ask asylum
In the swine.
The gentleness of God—
Not wrath, not tyranny,
Not vengeful rage
Determined to destroy—
But gentleness.

All the vast power of heaven
Breathed in You
So gently
That the smoking flax could burn,
The reed not break
And those who crucified You
Be forgiven
For love's sake.

3/1/87

Army

We, the world's wounded,
Bleeding, unaware,
Walking through weary wars
On broken feet,
Stumble across your love
And prostrate there
Lose all our pain in yours,
Our victim sweet!

8/15/78

Hurting

Only pierced hands
Are gentle enough
To touch some wounds.
The quivering flesh
Shrinks even from love,
Yet knows
That without this touch
There can be no healing.
How can one reach
A deeply hidden hurt
Without revealing
A massiveness of pain
That makes the helper
Cringe in dismay?
You need
To have been crucified yourself
If you would find the tenderness
To stay and share the pain
Again and yet again.

11/25/79

Upholding

The cross could not cry out,
It simply held Him there.
Silent supporter of Him
In His pain,
It stood
Mute, helpless, wood.

I feel as helpless as the cross
To stop your pain,
Can only hold you
When it comes again,
Be with you
In this hurt I can't prevent
And hold you
Till your suffering is spent.

5/11/87

The Cross

Dark, barren trunk,
Strong tree,
Your massiveness and might
O'ershadow me.

Blind to Your mercies, Lord,
I feared Your shade.
I tried to live
Only in sunshine.
You have made
Both light and darkness.
Both are filled with You.

I seek Your light
But need Your darkness, too.

8/27/78

Wings

Bound to my cross
I soar
Winging
The star-swept sky.
The burden
I had feared before
Bears me on high.

8/17/78

Dead and Buried

And so we took Him down
(Or thought we did),
Wiped off the sweat and spittle
From His face,
Washed the dried blood,
Threw out the crown of thorns,
And wrapped Him once again
In swaddling clothes.

A tomb can be
A cramped, confining place,
Far smaller than a stable.
We laid Him there
(Or thought we did).
We were not able to comprehend
The infinite contained.
For us, it was the end.
Only the harsh realities
Of death and stone
Remained.

4/10/82

Easter Saturday

A curiously empty day,
As if the world's life
Had gone underground.
The April sun
Warming dry grass
Makes pale spring promises
But nothing comes to pass.

Anger
Relaxes into despair
As we remember our helplessness,
Remember Him hanging there.
We have purchased the spices
But they must wait for tomorrow.
We shall keep today
For emptiness
And sorrow.

4/5/80

Gardens

Even in hot dry lands
Gardens are cool at dawn,
Heavy with dew,
Expectant,
Anointing with their fragrance
Those who come
On heavy-hearted errands
For the dead.

They had spent the Sabbath in grief
And in wondering why.
Now in the waning dark,
Timorous, faithful,
Reassuring each other,
They came to be true to Him.
And there in the quiet green,
The universe opened around them.

7/16/79

Mary

The Love I love
Came in the early dawning,
Standing as still as light.

How could I ever have dreamed
So sweet a morning
After so dark a night?

4/10/82

Opening

Now is the shining fabric of our day
Torn open, flung apart,
Rent wide by Love.
Never again
The tight, enclosing sky,
The blue bowl,
Or the star-illumined tent.
We are laid open to infinity,
For Easter Love
Has burst His tomb and ours.
Now nothing shelters us
From God's desire—
Not flesh, not sky,
Not stars, not even sin.
Now Glory waits
So He can enter in.
Now does the dance begin.

4/20/81

Explosiveness

What power could compress a universe
To pinhead size
And then explode it far beyond our skies,
So that our eyes,
Even with aids,
Cannot begin to trace
The constantly expanding edge of space?
What power did this?
Why, the self-same power
That comes to break apart
The tight-locked hardness
Of the human heart.

7/8/92

Dying/Rising

There comes a moment
When we lay aside
Life's winding sheets
And, springing from the tomb,
Of flesh, time, space,
Go forth
To meet our Lover
Face to face.

9/6/87

Conqueror

Sometime,
I'd like to meet the angel who
Not only rolled away the stone
But sat upon it too.

He demonstrated once for all
That death's inferior,
By placing on the tomb's dread stone
His heavenly posterior.

4/22/86

Larks Rising

(For Sister Jane Cicely CHN)

I love the thought
That we can sing and praise,
Mounting like larks
Throughout our common days,
Until at last we rise
Beyond the confines
Of these mortal skies,
And singing, praising
Soar
Straight into Paradise
To sing for evermore.

3/31/86

Repentance

Scour my soul with the winds of spring.
Wash me with April rain.
Set me out in your sun to dry,
And make me clean again.

4/11/81

Prescient

You made the quilted quiet
Of the woods,
Made trunks and branches,
Made the buds of spring,
The deep cool green of summer
And the tall profusion
Of bright color in the fall.

Now in the early spring,
The trees stand still,
Their buds close folded
Waiting for the sun.
But deep within
They know your holy will.
The sap is rising,
Easter has begun.

4/12/87

Artist

I have known God
During winter's silence and stone,
Have clung to the pure bone
Of the harsh, white cold.

And now?
Now He makes Himself known
In bird and blossom and blade.
The joyous abundance of spring
Dazzles and deafens.

If all this ecstasy is only spring
In one small part of one small planet,
What must You be like,
Maker of everything?

5/16/79

Tongues

Oh, lonely singer in the mystic dawn,
Facing the sun
And pouring out your heart
In flaming tongues of song,
How beautiful you are!

Standing above the trees,
You hail the Lord
Who rises in the fullness of His love
To free the song in each of us.

Now may we all
Turn toward the dawn, the light,
And let our God reveal
Himself all bright—
A shining, singing loveliness
Of glory, mercy, might!

10/2/79

Heaven or Earth?

Lord, if I died in early spring,
How would I know
Whether or not I had,
When all things here below
Are filled with life and light
Enough for heaven.

Lord, when I'm filled with spring
And have succumbed to her sweet spell,
How can I tell whether I'm still on earth
Or new arrived in heaven?

Creator of this world's bright beauty,
May I be forgiven
If I mistake Your lovely earth
For heaven.

3/6/94

Moon Magic

There came a night in April
When the moon
Hung like a golden globe
Above the trees.
Light lay along the land
Soft as the bloom on fruit.

The black cat sneaked and streaked
Across the grass,
Only his Siamese shadow
Matching leap for leap
As velvet moved through silver.

Was I asleep?
Was so much beauty real
Or did I dream?
I rose as in a dream
Mounting the golden beam
Up to the hole in the sky
Where the light comes through.

I should have said, "Goodbye."
This dream may last
For an eternity or two.

4/16/79

Pegasus?

And did I only fancy that I sat
Athwart those mighty shoulders?
Only imagine that I felt
The lift and thrust of those gigantic wings?
My thighs remember the muscular ripple and swell
Of swiftness and strength beyond our usual knowing.
How can I tell whether I dreamed?
I must go and look at the earth and the grass.
Perhaps I will find a hoof print,
Some sign that it did come to pass.
Perhaps I will find
Only the echoes of my own imaginings.

3/13/79

Memory

Your coat was blue, bright blue.
The cherry blossoms floated
Across the vividness of you.
Years intervened. I moved.
You died, they say.
But still I see
The petals in your hair
That April day.

7/8/79

May

May Morning

There's a silver star
And a cloud's turned pink.
It's the loveliest time in the world,
I think—
A morning in May
When the day is new
And the rising sun's just breaking through.
The light spreads gold
On the leaves of spring
And the birds
And my heart
Begin to sing.

5/29/85

Early

A moth began the morning.
He fluttered on my sill,
His voice so soft
I'd scarce have heard
Except the air were still.

A spider web
Was clothed in mist,
The grass, bejeweled with dew,
A robin spoke politely
And then, the sun broke through.

6/11/86

The Way Life Works

Buds are made to uncurl,
Sails and flags, to unfurl.
A chrysalis must open
To release a butterfly.

We fear this law of birth
That animates our earth
And shrink within our shells,
Wishing that God had made
Some less demanding plan
And not asked so much openness
Of man.

9/28/78

A Rose

A rose is silk and velvet
Come alive,
Moist, dewy, scented,
Beautiful as love.
A rose begins
Small, hard, closed in upon,
Sheltered by thorns.
We watch it opening,
Responding to the touch
Of warmth and sun
Petal by petal
Till its golden heart
Lies naked and exposed
To light, to bees
To every passerby.
What giving of itself
For one so shy!
Yet in this giving
It becomes full rose
Before it has to die.

6/25/90

Butterfly

Shall I stay coward
And cocooned
Or hazard my fragility
On the warm breath of Love?

The breeze may die
Or turn into a gale
Or simply float me
Toward some sunlit place
Where life is warm
And nectared.

Trust!
I can only trust.
There is no way of knowing
Before my going.

6/20/82

Power

There is in every child
A kind of light,
A sparkle of expectancy.
They look at life with hope,
Ecstatic over kittens,
Easter eggs,
Butterflies, ice cream, sparklers,
Baby pigs.
And we, who make the rules,
Can nourish their delight
Or use our power to dim it,
Snuff it out.
We hold them in our hands,
Candles of joy
Whose brightness we can nurture
Or destroy.

12/18/79

Cartwheels

Head down in a green sky
Starred with dandelions,
I wheel across the wheeling world.
I am bursting with green,
With the sap and the juice
And the youth of it.

I wheel and I feel
The springing stems, the urgency.
I am sprinkled and spangled
With yellow.
Spring-spangled
With spring gold.

5/14/79

Spring Promenade

The maple's wearing scarlet,
The birch chose palest green,
The lilac's royal purple
Would benefit a queen.

The white oak's decked in dusky pink,
Wild plum's a bridal white.
The poplar's shimmering in gold,
The beech, in copper bright.

Caparisoned in blossom,
The trees all dance for spring.
They flirt beneath the Maytime moon
And sway and bow and sing.

5/5/83

Pines

Patterns of pine
Against the sky
Are curiously soothing
To the eye
And, if persistently observed,
Provide
A kind of cool, green
Peacefulness
Inside.

6/11/86

Peace

Still! So still!
The robin gathers insects in the grass.
Clouds move across the sun
And then are gone.
A lady bug advances toward my chair.
The dogs sleep quietly
And there is silence everywhere.

Things settle and I watch them falling.
The duties of the day drift by,
The disappointments and the joys.
They are remote now
And the noise they made
Is now quite past recalling.

Our Shepherd bids them cease,
And in His pastures
I lie down in peace.

8/21/96

My Eden

I would be
Like a watered garden
For the Lord—
My roots, deep in His goodness,
My leaves, green with His grace.
I would
That He would create in me
A space
Filled with His loveliness . . .
And that in the cool of the evening
He would come
And walk about the place.

5/29/80

Afterglow

Your giant quiet lingers in me, Lord,
Slows worry's quickened pulse
And soothes and stills
Habitual hurrying.
I breathe in harmony
With the great quiet bowl
Of the evening sky.
In the deep pools of consciousness,
Stars start to shine.
Somewhere hope wakes
And sings a sleepy note.
The stillness settles deeper
And I rest in You.

5/15/79

Moon Mirror

Cooled and reflected now,
The hidden sun
Gleams pale as silver
On the shadowed land.
We are not warmed
Yet we are reassured.
Somewhere the sun is shining!
Here, the steadfast stone
Reflects a glory greater than its own,
And promises of morning keep
Pouring around us while we sleep.

10/13/78

Meeting

The sweetness of God's presence flows.
Out of the chapel door it goes
And meets alyssum coming in
Whose sweetness born beneath the sun
Spreads where His sweetness had begun.

9/19/84

Retreat

Afloat on love,
Wings folded, effort stilled,
Riding the swells of peace,
In harmony
With all that You have willed.

8/12/78

Chapel

Sink singing into silence.
Love, draw near.
The blessed of the Lord
Are gathered here.

8/13/78

Healing

This is the valley
Where she brought her heart
After he'd broken it.
She needed quietness
So she could heal.
The valley knew the art
Of gentleness.
Its streams flowed clear,
Smoothing the stones
And comforting her ears.
Slowly, she too became
Alive and green again.

12/7/88

Stone Song

I am the song of the singing stone.
Listen!
I pour myself out in a musical stream
Of loving and laughter and tenderest dream.
I am the song of the singing stone.
Listen!

I am the voice of the singing stone.
Listen!
I carry the sound of the mothering sea
And the power of sunlight shouts in me.
I am the voice of the singing stone.
Listen!

I am the sound of the singing stone.
Listen!
You will hear in me the whisper of cloud,
The silence of shadow, the shudder of earth,
The joy that spoke at creation's birth.
I am the sound of the singing stone.
Listen!

2/22/86

Streams of Thought

When something's written right,
The flow of it
Should slip across the mind
As smoothly as the waters of a stream
Slide over well-worn stones.

The silver stream of sound
May part a bit,
Ripple a little here,
Run deeper there,
Clear and translucent,
Till it gleams from sight.

Every word moves as sweetly
As clear water over stones,
When something's written right.

10/10/91

Haiku

Japanese patterns—
Words arranged
Precisely as blossoming branches.

4/10/86

Hatchling

Ideas, impressions, dreams,
Sensations, moods
Become the eggs
On which a poet broods
Hour after hour,
Turning them around.
It may be days, weeks, years
Before she hears
The tiny pecking sound
Of a shell opening
And truths emerging,
Born of some hidden urging.

2/5/90

Cream

From the white depths
The poem's richness rises
Clotting in thickened skins
Across my soul.

I rise and skim
The spirit-filled surprises
And fill with cream
The paper's empty bowl.

8/18/79

Animation

After a while,
They yawn and stretch and rise
And stand up by themselves.
We are surprised
That words can move about,
Make friends or enemies—
And start to live quite separate lives.
They seemed so insubstantial
When they came.
No longer flat and tame,
They rise up from the page
Like sudden flame.

3/8/93

Like Georgia O'Keeffe

I want to settle down
With my barrel of bones,
Sketch and resketch,
Describe, anatomize, portray
Until the essence of their boniness
Reaches across
From my hard skull to yours
And knocks into each one of us
The stark, essential, skeletal reality
Of bones.

3/17/86

A Trust

Poems?
Why, poems are like dreams,
Fragile as feathers,
Delicate as fern,
Pure as a flower is pure
Yet distant and obscure
As the land of dreams
When we have forgotten the dream.

They ring within your heart
Like the remembered echo of a bell.
If you carry within yourself
The slightest seed,
Even a single cell
Of poetry,
Cherish its potency
And guard it well.

5/9/80

Clarification

Touching of pen to page
Releases like a spring,
Or like the careful probing
Of a key in some old lock,
The hidden secrets
That the mind has held.
We are not sure
Just who we are
Or how we want to feel
Or what
Of all that claims to be Reality
Is real.
Sometimes, the act of writing
Can reveal
Which truths are true,
Which will defy corrosion, moth and rust,
And which, after so many years,
Have turned to dust.

9/4/84

Impressionist

Sometimes the sunlight is the message,
The sunlight
And the way the surf creeps up the sand.
Those, and the play of the light
On the hand
Of the woman holding the parasol.
Sometimes, the sunlight is the message—
But the artist doesn't need to explicate
His elaborate philosophy
At all.

9/11/89

Creation

Oh, poem,
You are so ephemeral!
I hold you tenderly
And try to catch your colors,
Not to bruise your wings.

Noise, interruptions, duties
Many things
Crowd in
And try to crush
The music of you.

Whenever there's a hush,
You flutter in me still and try to sing.

Oh, poem,
May I discipline my life
So that you can take wind,
Poem, I love you.

3/9/81

To an Artist

Spin, sister, spin!
The silk's all there
Inside you
Ready, stored.

Begin, only begin
Your dance among the stems
And weave anew
The special beauty
That comes forth from you.

Spin, side step, glide,
Drop down, creep up again.
Be bold,
Weaving the patterned beauty
God has told.
Begin,
Begin to spin!

4/2/86

For a Composer

It must be so exciting
When songs start to sing,
And you can hear
Within yourself
The music that will be.

Just as a bird detects
A chirp within the eggs
Beneath her breast,
Or as a pregnant woman feels
A heartbeat not her own,

So you must know
The thrill of giving birth,
Of bringing into life
A beauty never known before
On earth.

6/4/86

Menotti Music

The feathered fingers brush the keys
Unlocking faintest melodies.
Sudden cacophony of brassy triumph
Rears shining, swells its golden sides,
And cries exulting through the skies,
While violin begins to spin
Sound threads so thin
Their lace barely touches my face.

3/17/59

Quest

Leap the tall hedges
That enclose your mind
And ride your winged dreams
Into the far, far reaches of the sky.

Leave far behind
The small things you were sure of.
Go and find
The "things in heaven and earth"
Which this old world
Has not imagined yet.

Go
And do not forget
To bring back moons and miracles
So we who stay at home
Can also start to see.

12/6/88

Epitaph

I hope it will be said
When I am dead,
"She wrote good poems
And she made good bread."

But let it not be said
Till I am dead.
To say it now
Would surely turn my head.

1/23/78